ISBN 978-0-265-96520-7
PIBN 10916576

CATALOGUE

OF THE

UNIVERSITY OF THE NORTHWEST,

LOCATED AT

SIOUX CITY, IOWA.

————

1890–1891.

Press:
FORD BROTHERS
Sioux City.

THE UNIVERSITY OF THE NORTHWEST.

REV. WILMOT WHITFIELD, D. D., PRESIDENT.

BOARD OF MANAGERS.

REV. WILMOT WHITFIELD, D. D., President.
E. C. PETERS, Vice-President.   REV. R. C. GLASS, 2d Vice-Prest.
IRA N. PARDEE, Secretary.   A. S. GARRETSON, Treasurer.
ED. HAAKINSON,   EDWARD TODD,
J. F. HOPKINS,   ALEX. ELLIOTT,
JAS. A. JACKSON,   REV. WM. WHITFIELD.
GEO. EISENTRAUT.

IRA N. PARDEE, Financial Agent.
(Address, Sioux City, Iowa.)

EXECUTIVE COMMITTEE.

E. C. PETERS,   EDWARD TODD,
WILMOT WHITFIELD, D. D.   R. C. GLASS, A. M.
IRA N. PARDEE,   JAS. A. JACKSON.

AUDITING COMMITTEE.

E. C. PETERS,   JAS. A. JACKSON,
GEO. EISENTRAUT.

LAW COMMITTEE.

WILMOT WHITFIELD,   J. F. HOPKINS,
ED. HAAKINSON,   WILLIAM WHITFIELD.

BOARD OF REGENTS.

REV. G. W. L. BROWN,   -   -   Rock Rapids.
REV. J. W. LOTHIAN,   -   -   Correctionville.
REV. F. E. DAY.   -   -   -   -   Marcus.
REV. R. SMYLIE,   -   -   -   Cherokee.
HON. J. C. LOCHLIN,   -   -   -   Aurelia.
JOSEPH SAMPSON,   -   -   -   Sioux City.
C. B. OLDFIELD,   -   -   -   Sioux City.

THE UNIVERSITY OF THE NORTHWEST.

GENERAL FACULTY.

WILMOT WHITFIELD, D. D., Chancellor.

R. C. GLASS, A. M.. S. T. B., Dean of College of Liberal Arts.   Professor of Mental and Moral Philosophy.

JOHN H. McGIBBONS, A. M., Professor of Greek and Latin.

H. G. PITTENGER, A. M., Professor of Chemistry and Natural Sciences.

MISS ANNA S. JENKINS, A B., Professor of French and German.

E. A. BROWN, Ph. B., Professor of Mathematics.

H. W. L. MAHOOD, A. B., Professor of History and English Literature.

MISS BESSIE M. McKICHAN, Instructor in Latin and Greek.

F. M. HARDING, B. S., B. D., Dean of College of Commerce.   Professor of Political Economy and Science of Accounts.

M. K. BUSSARD, Professor of Penmanship and Typewriting.

MISS JULIA M. FAY, Professor of Stenography.

G. A. BEACH, Instructor in Phonography.

E. S. JOHNSON, Instructor in Stenography.

J. C. GILCHRIST, A. M., Dean of College of Didactics.   Professor of Didactics.

MRS. F. M. HARDING, Professor of Elocution and Oratory.

EDWIN J. STASON, LL. B., Secretary of Law Department, Professor of Contracts and Torts.

J. W. HALLAM, LL. B., Professor of Real Property and Equity.

...., Professor of Pleading, Practice and Evidence.

HON. GIFFORD S. ROBINSON, (Associate Justice of the Supreme Court.) Lecturer on Constitutional Limitations.

HON. G. W. WAKEFIELD, (Judge of District Court.)   Lecturer on Conflict of Laws.

HON. C. H. LEWIS, (Judge of District Court.)   Lecturer on Preparation and Trial of Causes.

HON. E. H. HUBBARD, A. M., Lecturer on Extraordinary Legal Remedies.

C. L. WRIGHT, Lecturer on Corporations.

W. E. GANTT, Lecturer on Federal Jurisprudence.

...., Lecturer on Criminal Law.

A. S. WILSON, Lecturer on Insurance.

A. L. HUDSON, LL. B., Lecturer on Evidence.

A. F. CALL, Lecturer on Legal Study and Ethics.

MRS. EMILIE MALLORY, Director of Conservatory of Music, and Professor of Pianoforte and Organ.

MISS CARRIE B. OSGOOD, Instructor in Vocal Music.

MISS ALICE B. GUNN, Assistant Instructor in Music.

GEORGE W. BEGGS, A. M., M. D., Sioux City, Dean, Professor of Clinical Surgery.

E. HORNABROOKE, M. D., Cherokee, Iowa, Professor of Theory and Practice of Medicine and Clinical Medicine.

GENERAL FACULTY.—Continued.

JOHN P. SAVAGE, M. D., Sioux City, Professor of Obstetrics, Gynecology and Surgical Diseases of Women.

J. A. SHERMAN, M. D., Cherokee, Iowa, Professor of Theory and Practice of Surgery.

H. A. WHEELER, M. D., Onawa, Iowa, Professor of Materia Medica and Therapuetics.

WILLIAM JEPSON, M. D., Sioux City, Professor of Anatomy, Assistant to Professor of Clinical Surgery, and Secretary of Faculty.

J. H. TALBOY, M. D., Castana, Iowa, Professor of Physiology and Histology.

GEORGE PARK, M. B., C. M., Sioux City, Professor of Ophthalmology and Otology.

H. G. PITTENGER, A. M., Sioux City, Professor of Chemistry and Toxicology.

M. W. WHITE, M. D., Sioux City, Professor of Diseases of Children.

S. B. INGALLS, M. D., Meridan, Iowa, Professor of Pathology and Bacteriology.

W. D. HASSON, M. D., Norfolk, Neb , (Physician to the Nebraska Hospital for Insane), Lecturer on Insanity.

GEORGE JEPSON, LL. B., Sioux City, Lecturer on Medical Jurisprudence.

W. S. THARP, M. D., Sioux City, Lecturer on Genito-Urinary Diseases.

E. D. FREAR, M. D., Sloan, Iowa, Lecturer on Dermatology.

S. C. HATCH, D. D. S., Sioux·City, Lecturer on Dental Science.

GUY C. RICH, M. D., Sioux City, Demonstrator of Anatomy and Curator of the Medical Museum.

General Information.

The UNIVERSITY OF THE NORTHWEST is located on beautiful grounds on Morningside, the most delightful suburb of Sioux City, from which a commanding view is had of the city and surrounding country. The broad Missouri sweeps away to the west and south under the eye of the beholder, while the landscape stretches away in endless beauty, in some directions to a distance of twenty-five miles, including portions of three states in the splendid panorama. Many competent judges pronounce this the finest college site in this country. For beauty and healthfulness, nothing more could be desired.

The University is reached from the city by the elevated railway, and ere long the Morningside extension of the electric railway will run to the campus.

MORAL CULTURE.

While this institute is under the fostering care of the Methodist Episcopal Church, it is free from sectarianism, and will be conducted on broad christian principles. The management of the University is firmly persuaded that there can be no symmetrical character formed without proper culture being given to the moral and religious faculties. This is a fact that will be kept prominently before the minds of the students in all our intercourse with them, and in the various rules and regulations of the institution. The Faculty will seek in all proper ways to inculcate the truth, that the highest possible success is only to be attained by a life conformed to all the revealed will of God.

We therefore require of all our students to attend upon the religious services at the chapel at the opening of each school day, and on the Sabbath morning services of such church as they, or their

parents or guardians may select.   Also on the Sabbath numerous
bible classes will be conducted by members of the Faculty at which
the students are earnestly counseled to be present.   In these and
other ways the moral and religious life of the student will be carefully
fostered.

GOVERNMENT.

We believe that the best government is self government.   Hence
the institution has no long code of rules, but a few simple requirements that will commend themselves to all right minded persons.
Our students therefore will, in a large measure, be placed upon their
honor, the Faculty simply insisting upon such conduct as becomes
their high position as students of a christian college.   Our University
is not a reform school; hence persons whose conduct is detrimental to
the school, and does not yield to the affectionate counsels of the
Faculty will be dismissed from the institution.   Punctual atten'dance
upon the duties of the school, and a careful observance of study
hours is expected.

As the University is open alike to ladies and gentlemen, great
care will be taken that no improprieties are committed, in their general deportment towards each other, and the visiting and association
of ladies and gentlemen is strictly forbidden, except at such times
and under such regulations as the Faculty may deem wise.

Everything in deportment which interferes with the highest
mental and moral development of the student is prohibited, such as
profanity, obscenity, gambling, the playing of cards and billiards, the
use of intoxicating liquors, and all forms of disipation.   The use of
tobacco in the buildings or upon the grounds of the University is forbidden.   This is required because of the presence of ladies and others to whom it is offensive, and because the habit is expensive, as
well as uncleanly, and detrimental to health.

Those who cannot cheerfully be governed by these simple and
just requirements are advised to seek elsewhere.

EXPENSES.

It has been the earnest purpose of the management of the University to bring the expenses of the student within the smallest limits
possible consistent with a high-grade institution.

Tuition in the College of Liberal Arts will be $12 per term and the incidental fee $6. In the Preparatory Department the tuition will be $9 per term and the incidental fee $5. Students in Chemistry will be charged $6 per term for breakage and material used. The diploma fee will be $6. For tuition in other departments, see such departments.

Board in the Dining Hall will be $2.25 per week. Rooms furnished with bedstead, bed spring, mattress, commode, toilet set, chairs, table and carpet will be rented to each of two students for prices ranging from 50 cents to $1.00 per week, according to location. If one person occupies the room alone, the price will be double. Board and neatly furnished rooms in private families will range in price from $2.75 to $3.50 per week. Students who board themselves can still further reduce the cost of living.

Preparatory Department.

GENERAL PLAN.

This department has four courses of study, extending through three years each, and corresponding with and fitting the student for the respective courses of study in the College of Liberal Arts. These preparatory courses are as follows: Classical, Philosophical, Scientific and Modern Literature.

REQUIREMENTS FOR ADMISSION.

The applicant for admission to this department must be at least *thirteen* years of age, and possess such proficiency as to be able to complete English Grammer in two terms, Arithmetic in one term, History of the United States in one term, and Geography in one term. Persons qualified by previous study to take advanced standing will be classified accordingly. Every facility will be accorded to students of mature age to complete their preparation as speedily as desirable. A certificate of good moral character from former teachers, or others, will be required of those who seek admission. It will be greatly to the advantage of those desiring to begin the study of any language to enter the school in September.

Persons desiring to pursue special studies in English, Mathematics, History and the Sciences may enter at any time and find classes suited to their wants.

Examination for admission to the preparatory course will be held on the day previous to the day of opening each term. Persons presenting satisfactory certificates from other schools or colleges, showing character and amount of work done, will be admitted so far as those studies are concerned without further examination.

COURSES OF STUDY—PREPARATORY DEPARTMENT.

FIRST YEAR.

	Classical.	Philosophical.	Scientific.	Modern Literature.
1st TERM.	1 Latin—Grammar Lessons. 2 English--Grammar 3 Mathematics—Arithmetic finished.	1 Latin—Grammar Lessons. 2 English—Grammar. 3 Matematics—Arithmetic finished.	1 Latin—Grammar Lessons. 2 English—Grammar. 3 Mathematics–Arithmetic finished.	1 Latin—Grammar lessons. 2 English—Grammar. 3 Mathematics—Arithmetic finished.
2d TERM.	1 Latin—Grammar Lessons. 2 Physiology—Human 3 English—Grammar	1 Latin—Grammar Lessons. 2 Physiology—Human 3 English—Grammar.	1 Latin—Grammar lessons. 2 Physiology–Human. 3 English—Grammar.	1 Latin—Grammar lessons. 2 Physiology-Human. 3 English—Grammar.
3d TERM.	1 Latin—Grammar Cæsar. 2 Geography–Physical 3 History—History of the United States.	1 Latin—Grammar Cæsar. 2 Geography–Physical 3 History—History of the United States	1 Latin—Grammar Cæsar. 2 Geography–Physical 3 History—History of the United States.	1 Latin—Grammar Cæsar. 2 Geography–Physical 3 History—History of the United States.

SECOND YEAR.

	Classical.	Philosophical.	Scientific.	Modern Literature.
1st TERM.	1 Latin—Grammar; Cæsar, composition. 2 Mathematics—A gebra. 3 Physics—Dynamics.	1 Latin—Grammar; Cæsar, Composition. 2 Mathematics—Algebra. 3 Physics—Dynamics.	1 French—Grammar; lessons. 2 Mathematics—Algebra. 3 Zoology—Elements.	1 French — Grammar; lessons. 2 Mathematics—Algebra. 3 History—History of England.
2d TERM.	1 Latin—Grammar; Cicero. 2 History—History of Greece. 3 Mathematics—Algebra.	1 Latin—Grammar; Cicero. 2 History—History of Greece. 3 Mathematics—Algebra.	1 French—Grammar; lessons. 2 Astronomy–Descriptive. 3 Mathematics—Algebra.	1 French — Grammar; lessons. 2 History--History of Greece. 3 Mathematics—Algebra.
3d TERM.	1 Latin—Grammar; Ovid. 2 History—History of Rome. 3 Mathematics—Algebra.	1 Latin—Grammar; Ovid. 2 History—History of Rome. 3 Mathematics—Algebra.	1 French — Grammar; lessons. 2 Botany—Systematic. 3 Mathematics—Algebra.	1 French — Grammar; lessons. 2 History—History of Rome. 3 Mathematics—Algebra. br.

THIRD YEAR.

	Classical	Philosophical	Scientific	Modern Literature
1st TERM.	1 Latin—Virgil; Prosody; composition. 2 Greek—Anabasis; Grammar; composition. 3 Mathematics—Geometry.	1 Latin—Virgil; Prosody; composition. 2 Mathematics—Geometry. 3 French. 4 Drawing.	1 German—Grammar; lessons. 2 Mathematics—Geometry. 3 Physics—Dynamics. 4 Drawing.	1 German—Grammar; lessons. 2 Mathematics — Geometry. 3 Physics—Dynamics. 4 Drawing.
2d TERM.	1 Latin—Virgil. 2 Greek—Anabasis; Grammar; Composition. 3 Mathematics—Geometry.	1 Latin—Virgil. 2 Mathematics—Geometry. 3 French. 4 Drawing.	1 German—Grammar; lessons; 2 Mathematics—Geometry. 3 Physics—Electricity. 4 Drawing.	1 German—Grammar; lessons. 2 Mathematics — Geometry. 3 Physics—Electricity. 4 Drawing.
3d TERM.	1 Latin—Cicero. 2 Greek—Iliad; Prosody. 3 Mathematics—Algebra; Geometry reviewd.	1 Latin—Cicero. 2 Mathematics—Algebra; Geometry reviewed. 3 French. 4 Drawing.	1 German— Grammar; lessons. 2 Mathematics—Algebra; Geometry reviewd. 3 Physics-Heat, Light and Sound. 4 Drawing.	1 German—Grammar; lessons. 2 Mathematics—Algebra; Geometry reviewd. 3 Botany—Systematic. 4 Drawing.

COLLEGE OF LIBERAL ARTS.

FACULTY.

———

Wilmot Whitfild, D. D., President.

R. C. Glass, A. M., S. T. B., Dean,
Professor of Mental and Moral Science.

J. H. McGibbons, A. M.,
Professor of Greek and Latin Languages and Literature.

Miss Anna B. Jenkins, A. B.,
Professor of French and German.

E. A. Brown, Ph. B.,
Professor of Mathematics and Astronomy.

H. W. L. Mahood, A. B.,
Professor of History and English Literature.

H. G. Pittenger, A. M.,
Professor of Physics and Chemistry.

Miss Bessie M. McKichan,
Instructor in Greek and Latin.

College of Liberal Arts.

COURSES OF STUDY.

The College of Liberal Arts presents four courses of study each requiring four year's work to complete it, namely: The Classical course, the Philosophical course, the Scientific course, and the course in Modern Literature.

CLASSICAL COURSE.

In the first and second years of this course special prominence is given to Greek and Latin. Two years in Greek and three in Latin are necessary to admission. In the

PHILOSOPHICAL COURSE

Greek is omitted and Latin is made elective after the Freshman year. More time is given to the study of the Modern languages, Mathematics and Sciences. In the

SCIENTIFIC COURSE

French and German take the place of Greek and Latin, and great prominence is given to Mathematics, Natural and Physical Science. In the

COURSE IN MODERN LITERATURE

The Modern languages are substituted for the Classics, and in connection with the study of the Sciences, much time is given to History and English Literature.

TERMS OF ADMISSION.

Students desiring admission to the Freshman class in any one of the courses named above must be prepared to pass an examination in the various studies required in the corresponding courses as laid down in the preparatory department as given in another part of this catalogue.

A certificate of good moral character is also required, and if the student comes from another college, a certificate of honorable dismissal.

SPECIAL STUDIES.

Arrangements will be made for the accommodation of those who do not seek a degree, but desire to pursue special studies in this department.

Each professor will judge of the fitness of the applicant to pursue special branches in his department.

Special students will be required to conform to the same rules of order as regular students, in regard to attendance upon chapel services, public worship, and rhetorical exercises, unless specially excused.

Such students who have pursued special studies with success for at least six terms will be entitled to a certificate.

EXAMINATIONS.

Examinations for admission to the College of Liberal Arts will be held on the Monday preceding commencement, and on the Tuesday next before the opening of the college year. Persons may be examined and admitted at other times, but they are earnestly advised to enter at the beginning of the year. Candidates for admission to the Freshman class must be at least *sixteen* years of age.

COLLEGIATE DEPARTMENT—COURSES OF STUDY.

FRESHMAN CLASS.

	Classical.	Philosophical.	Scientific.	Modern Literature.
1st Term.	1 Greek—Orations of Lysias; composition. 2 Latin—Cicero; composition. 3 Mathematics—Solid Geometry; Algebra.	1 Latin—Cicero; composition. 2 French Literature. 3 Mathematics—Solid Geometry; Algebra.	1 German Literature. 2 French Literature. 3 Mathematics—Solid Geometry; Algebra.	1 German Literature. 2 French Literature. 3 Mathematics—Solid Geometry; Algebra.
2d Term	1 Greek—Herodotus. 2 Latin—Livy. 3 Mathematics—Algebra; Trigonometry.	1 Latin—Livy; c'mp's'n 2 French Literature. 3 Mathematics—Algebra; Trigonometry.	1 German Literature. 2 French Literature. 3 Mathematics—Algebra; Trigonometry.	1 German Literature. 2 French Literature. 3 Mathematics—Algebra; Trigonometry.
3d Term	1 Greek—The Odyssey. 2 Latin—Horace. 3 Mathematics—Trigonometry.	1 Latin—Horace. 2 French Literature. 3 Mathematics—Trigonometry.	1 German Literature. 2 French Literature. 3 Mathematics—Trigonometry.	1 German Literature. 2 French Literature. 3 Mathematics—Trigonometry.

SOPHOMORE CLASS.

	Classical	Philosophical	Scientific	Modern Literature
1st Term.	1 Greek. 2 Latin. 3 German—Grammar; selections.	1 French Literature. 2 German—Grammar; selections. 3 English Literature; composition.	1 Mathematics—Determinants and Graphic Algebra. 2 Chemistry. 3 German Literature.	1 French Literature. 2 German Literature. 3 English Literature and composition.
2d Term	1 Greek. 2 Latin. 3 German Literature.	1 French Literature. 2 German Literature. 3 Mathematics—Analytical Geometry.	1 Mathematics—Analytical Geometry. 2 Chemistry. 3 German Literature.	1 French Literature. 2 German Literature. 3 English Literature and composition.
3d Term	1 Greek. 2 Latin or 3 German. 4 Botany.	1 Botany. 2 German Literature. 3 Rhetoric. (2). 4 English Literature. (3)	1 Mathematics—Calculus. 2 Chemistry 3 Anatomy.	1 Anatomy. 2 Rhetoric (3) and Elecution. (2). 3 English Literature and composition.

JUNIOR CLASS.

	Classical.	Philosophical.	Scientific.	Modern Literature.
1st Term.	1 Physics. 2 Logic. 3 History or 4 Chemistry or 5 Calculus.	1 Logic. 2 Physics. 3 History or 4 Chemistry or 5 Calculus.	1 Physics. 2 Logic. 3 History or 4 Integral Calculus or 5 Chemistry.	1 Logic. 2 History. 3 Chemistry or 4 Physics or 5 Calculus.
2d Term.	1 Metaphysics. 2 Physics. 3 Zoology or 4 History or 5 Chemistry.	1 Metaphysics. 2 Physics. 3 Zoology. 4 History or 5 Chemistry.	1 Physics. 2 Zoology. 3 History or 4 Metaphysics or 5 Chemistry.	1 Metaphysics. 2 History. 3 Zoology or 4 Physics or 5 Chemisry.
3d Term.	1 Metaphysics. 2 Physics. 3 Geology or 4 History or 5 Chemistry.	1 Metaphysics. 2 Physics. 3 Geology or 4 History or 5 Chemistry.	1 Physics. 2 Geology. 3 Chemistry or 4 Metaphysics or 5 History.	1 Metaphysics. 2 History. 3 Geology or 4 Physics or 5 History.

SENIOR CLASS.

	Classical.	Philosophical.	Scientific.	Modern Literature.
1st Term	1 Ethics. 2 Political Economy. 3 History or 4 Biology or 5 English Literature or 6 Physics.	1 Ethics. 2 Political Economy. 3 Geology or 4 History or 5 Biology or 6 Chemistry.	1 Ethics. 2 Physics. 3 Geology or 4 Political Economy or 5 Biology or 6 History.	1 Ethics. 2 Political Economy. 3 Geology or 4 History or 5 Biology or 6 Physics.
2d Term	1 Christian Evidences. 2 Constitutional Law. 3 Astronomy or 4 History or 5 Greek Testament or 6 Political Economy.	1 Christian Evidences. 2 Constitutional Law. 3 Astronomy or 4 History or 5 Political Economy or 6 Biology.	1 Christian Evidences. 2 Astronomy. 3 Political Economy or 4 Constitutional L'w or 5 Biology or 6 History.	1 Christian Evidences. 2 Constitutional Law. 3 Political Economy or 4 Biology or 5 History or 6 Astronomy.
3d Term	1 Natural Theology. 2 Butler's Analogy. 3 Hist'y of Civiliza'n or 4 International Law or 5 Astronomy or 6 Greek Testament.	1 Natural Theology. 2 History of Civilizat'n 3 Butler's Analogy or 4 International Law or 5 Astronomy or 6 Practical Physics.	1 Natural Theology. 2 Astronomy. 3 History of Civilizat'n 4 Biology or 5 International Law or 6 Practical Physics.	1 Natural Theology. 2 History of Civilizat'n 3 International Law or 4 Astronomy or 5 Biology or 6 English Literature.

COLLEGE OF COMMERCE.

FACULTY.

REV. WILMOT WHITEFIELD, D. D. President,
> Political and Commercial Ethics.

F. H. HARDING, B. S. B. D. Dean,
> Science of Accounts, Political Economy, Parlimentary Law.

A. E. BROWN, Ph. B.,
> Commercial Arthmetic and Rapid Computations.

E. J. STASON, B. S. L. L. B.,
> Civil Government and Law of Contracts.

M. K. BUSSARD,
> Penmanship, Type-writing, Business and Social Correspondence.

A. L. HUDSON, L. L. B.,
> Commercial Paper and Bailment.

MISS JULIA M. FAY,
> Stenography and Expert Type-writing.

G. A. BEACH,
> Phonography and the uses of Phonograph and Phonograph-Graphophone Machines.

E. S. JOHNSON,
> Assistant instructor in Stenography and Correspondence.

College of Commerce.

COURSE OF STUDIES.

FIRST TERM.

Book-keeping, Commercial Law, Commercial Arithmetic, Penmanship, Letter-writing.

SECOND TERM.

Book-keeping, Commercial Law, Commercial Arithmetic, Civil Government, Penmanship.

THIRD TERM.

Actual Business Practice, Political Economy, Parliamentary Law, Parliamentary Practice.

PREPARATORY COURSE.,

Arithmetic, English Grammar, Composition, Geography, History of the United States, Penmanship.

SHORT-HAND AND TYPE-WRITING COURSE.

FIRST TERM.

Elementary Principles of Stenography, Word Signs, Phrasing, Dictation, Simple Exercises in Type-writing.

SECOND TERM.

Dictation, Amanuensis Work, Court Reporting, Expert Type-writing, Penmanship. .

PHONOGRAPH COURSE.

Use and care of the Phonograph, Expert Type-writing, Letter-writing, Penmanship.

REMARKS ON THE COURSE OF STUDY.

The educational features of each decade necessarily change to meet the changing demands of society.   This is pre-eminently a commercial age—nothing if not practical. As business life has its own laws, technical terms and peculiar methods of exchange, it becomes as essential that the business man have professional training as the physician, lawyer or theologian. There is no luck in business—knowledge is power. Business failures in nearly every instance are traceable to ignorance of the laws governing commercial transactions or violation of the ruling principles of trade.

That a knowledge of the technique is essential is self-evident but the failure of many of our business colleges to graduate successful men, is due to the fact that they recognize this qualification only and their graduates are at best only book-keepers. We believe that commercial education has assumed a wider field and this department of the University is designed to meet the demand. Its aim is to make business men, men who are not only competent book-keepers, but who are business managers, men who understand all the lines of business with which they are brought into contact, together with the laws which regulate and control them, men who are broad-minded and can come into successful competition with their fellowmen in the political and social as well the commercial realm.

BOOK-KEEPING.

The importence of this subject is not to be questioned. Our methods of instruction will be found superior to that adopted in ordinary commercial colleges. We require every student to have a thorough knowledge of the nature of each transaction before he records it and thus he is prevented from making incorrect entries.

Teaching precedes learning. We consider it a waste of time for a student simply to copy work to be submitted to his instructior for correction. Under such a plan a student becomes practically his own instructor and the errors which he commits will create a stronger impression upon his mind than the correction and thus become liable to repetition. To avoid such a result, all the details of each subject are thoroughly explained by the teacher in charge and transactions are then recorded by each student and reviewed the following day in recitation. The subjects of single and double entry, the complications of wholesale and retail merchandising, shipping, commission, insurance, banking, and all forms of investments, bills and discounts are thoroughly treated.

COMMERCIAL ARITHMETIC.

Thorough knowledge and correctness as well as rapidity are essential in business calculation. Supported by this belief, and with the idea of mental discipline always in view our course of study is unusually extensive, nor are we satisfied with mere mechanical work, we require each student to understand the "why as well as the how." We treat exhaustively the subjects of percentage, interest, discount, banking, profit and loss, shipping, commission, exchange, storage, insurance, taxes, duties, customs, general average, bankruptcy, partial payments, equation of payments, partnership, settlements, stocks and bonds, and marking goods, together with all rapid methods known to arithematical science.

PENMANSHIP.

We regard the importance of this subject beyond question, and consequently are prepared to give every student such instruction as will enable him to write legibly, rapidly and with ease. In this branch the student is given both class and individual instruction and by a systematic arrangement of movement exercises and analyses, the stiff, cramped, awkward hand is converted into one of legibility, rapidity and facility.

LETTER WRITING.

A business letter is of the utmost importance to its writer. It often precedes and introduces him or goes where he cannot, and upon its favorable or unfavorable impression depends the success of his business. Realizing this fact, we pay especial attention to this art, giving class instruction in composition, capitalizing, punctuation, etc., and practical drill wherever possible in connection with the routine work of the course, and also in the actual business practice.

COMMERCIAL LAW.

It is essential that the business man should understand the legal support belonging to him and the legal consequences of his transactions. To obtain this knowledge it is necessary that the student should make a study of the common law together with its statutory modifications relating to commercial transactions. This study need not include legal terms nor technicalities, nor need the student go as deeply into minutia as the student of law, otherwise his knowledge must be complete. In pursuing this study a comprehensive text-book including complete discussions of all laws relating to commercial subjects, is placed in the hands of each student. He is required not simply to listen to lectures or to be instructed in a few business forms; but lessons are assigned to him upon which he must study and think. The subject is taught by the topical method, with critical analysis and thorough discussions. The work in the practical department is so arranged that the student will have an opportunity to make an application of his knowledge.

CIVIL GOVERNMENT.

One of the requisites of a good business man is that he should be a good citizen, and to be a good citizen he must have a knowledge of the underlying principles of our government. In a government where every man has voice indirectly in making the laws, the danger of entrusting the powers of citizenship to ignorant persons has striking illustrations. In the study of this branch, as in every branch in this department, the student is required to pursue a complete course. He is first made acquainted with the forms of government, the origin and growth of our constitution, followed by a close analysis of our national, state and municipal governments, the details of elections, and appointments of home and foreign officers, and the minutia of legislative, executive and judicial departments.

POLITICAL ECONOMY.

No man can lay claim to thorough business qualification who does not possess a knowledge of the laws of Production, Consumption, Distribution, and Exchange; who does not understand the relations existing between Capital and Labor; Free Trade and Protective Tarif.

We shall in no wise teach political partisanism but shall endeavor to give the student a knowledge of the elementary principles of politics and political ethics and aid him in acquiring an unbiased and intelligent political judgment.

PARLIAMENTARY LAW.

How often and unexpectedly are men and women called upon to participate in the organization and continuation of public meetings, and how embarrassing the situation, and often how illegal the proceedings as a result of their ignorance of the laws and customs of such meetings. In this branch the student is instructed how to organize and conduct meetings of a social and business character; how officers are elected, sustained and removed; and all the details bearing upon motions, resolutions, etc.

PARLIAMENTARY PRACTICE.

In order that the student may have an opportunity to make application of the knowledge obtained from the study of Civil Government, Political Economy and Parliamentary Law, a system of parliamentary practice is put into operation in which all take an active part. A convention is organized in which students from all departments of the University may participate. Nominations are made, an election is held; a legislative department is organized, composed of a Senate and House of Representatives, which in turn elects such officers as are required and makes all necessary preparation for conducting congressional business; committees are appointed; bills introduced, recommended, passed or defeated. This work is not left entirely to inexperienced students, but is under the immediate charge of some member of the University Faculty.

ACTUAL BUSINESS DEPARTMENT.

Havin completed the theoretical work, the student is promoted to the Business Exchange Room, which is a representation of the business world. This department is equipped with eight large offices for counting-house work, and forty desks or smaller offices for retailing and shipping. Each student is furnished with manuscript work, and assigned a cash capital with which he conducts his business. All work is inspected by the instructor in charge who requires of the student that the books show at all times the real condition of his work. Nothing is permitted to pass that is not perfect in every respect.

The manuscript work being satisfactorily completed, the student is passed to the counting-house, entering first as collection or bill clerk and gradually working his way up to manager of the house. The student enters in turn the following offices: Wholesale House; Retail House, Commission, National Bank, Jobbing and Importing, Real Estate and Insurance, Rail Road Office, all of which are furnished with a full line of books and blanks of the most approved systems.

PREPARATORY COURSE.

In order to reach those who are not fully prepared to take up the work in the commercial course proper, a preparatory course has been arranged including instruction in the common English branches.

SHORTHAND AND TYPE-WRITING.

With the rapid increase of business comes the necessity for reporters, copyists, and type-writers. The demand for help in these lines was never so·great, nor so far from being supplied. So indispensable to business and professional men in this art, that young men and women possessing only a moderate degree of proficiency experience no difficulty in securing remunerative positions.

This course may be taken alone or in connection with other studies at the option of the student. It will be observed that the expenses in this course at the University of the ·Northwest are less than one-half those of other institutions devoted to these branches exclusively. Type-writing machines are furnished without extra charge.

PHONOGRAPHY.

This wonderful innovation has recently reached a state of perfection. It is rapidly coming into common use and in the near future will occupy an important place in the field of stenographic science. (See special circular.) To meet a certain demand, a course of study has been arranged including letter writing, type-writing and the mechanism of the Phonograph.

Time required, two months; tuition, $10. All machines for practice furnished without extra charge. This course may be taken alone or in connection with other studies.

TIME TO ENTER.

A year's work in this department of the University consists of four terms of twelve weeks each. Students will be admitted any time during the first week of each term, when new classes will be organized in all studies. Students found capable of doing more work than is found in the prescribed course may be promoted at the opening of each term.

TEXT BOOKS.

No new books need to be purchased, as a full line of text books for this department is kept on hand and will be rented to the student for a nominal sum.

EXPENSES.

Tuition $15 per term of twelve weeks payable in advance.

Table board $2.50 per week.

Furnished rooms from $0.50 to $1 per week.

Tuition for Shorthand and Type-writing $15 per term.

We ask that the expenses be compared with those of other Commercial Schools.

DIPLOMAS.

A diploma witih the seal of the University affixed, will be granted to all students who satisfactorily complete any one of the above courses.

CALENDER FOR 1890 AND 1891.

First term opens...........................September 1, 1890.

Second term opens.........................November 24, 1890.

Third   "   "   ....February 23, 1891.

Fourth   "   "   ....May 17, 1891.

COLLEGE OF DIDACTICS.
FACULTY.

———

Rev. Wilmot Whitfield, D. D., Chancellor.

J. C. Gilchrist, A. M., Dean,
             Professor of Didactics and Psychology.

E. A. Brown, Ph. B.,
             Professor of Mathematics.

M. K. Bussard,
             Professor of Penmanship.

J. S. Shoup,
             Lecturer on School Management.

Mrs. F. M. Harding,
             Teacher of Reading and Elocution.

Miss Carrie B. Osgood,
             Teacher of Vocal and Instrumental Music.

College of Didactics.

This College is organized for the thorough Professional Training of Teachers in all the Departments of the Science and Art of Education.

COURSE OF STUDY.

Those courses that have been developed by the experience of the best Normal Schools, State and Private, in our country during the past quarter of a century are adopted by the college of Didactics of the University.

There are five great divisions of knowledge constituting the Profession of Didactics, each of which will receive due consideration:

1. A knowledge of the Branches to be Taught.

2. A knowledge of the Approved Methods of Instruction.

3. A knowledge of the Organization and Administration of School Systems.

4. A knowledge of the Human Mind in all its conditions of Childhood, Youth and Manhood.

5. A knowledge of the History of Education.

The following table exhibits the Curriculum of these studies by terms and years, and is called the Didactic Course:

DIDACTIC COURSE OF STUDY.—UNIVERSITY OF THE NORTHWEST.

Departments.	FIRST YEAR. I TERM.	II TERM.	III TERM.	SECOND YEAR. I TERM.	II TERM.	III TERM.	THIRD YEAR. I TERM.	II TERM.	III TERM.	FOURTH YEAR.
Language.	English Grammar and Word Analysis.	English Grammar	Letter Writing and Composition	English Literature	*English Literature		Rhetoric			
Mathematics.	Arithmetic	Arithmetic	Book-Keeping	Algebra	Algebra	Algebra	Geometry	Geometry	Trigonometry Surveying	
Science.	Geography		Physiology	Physical Geography		Botany	Physics	*Physics	Chemistry	
History.		U. S. History of the United States	Constitution of the United States		Mediæval History	*Modern History	*Ancient History			
Art.	Penmanship and Drawing	Reading and Music Drawing	Penmanship and Drawing	Reading and Music Drawing	Penmanship and Drawing	Reading and Music	Drawing Perspective			
Didactics.	Lectures Theory of Education	Primary Methods	School Economy	Advanced Methods	Principles of Education	Graded Schools	Psychology	Psychology	History of Education	The true order of studies applied — Psychology — Philosophy of Education

Elective Studies from the College of Liberal Art.

Those subjects marked with a star are exchangeable with Latin. Classes in most of the Common Branches will be organized every term. For the most part, the Text Books in common use will be adopted.

GRADUATION AND DEGREES.

On the completion of the course, the student formally graduates and receives the degree of Bachelor of Didactics (B. D.)

Graduates will be deemed fitted to teach in all grades of the Public School System, and in the best High Schools.

POST GRADUATE COURSE.

Graduates of the Didactic Course who will spend one year in selected studies from any one of the four courses of the College of Liberal Arts, approved by the Faculty, and in addition a fourth year Didactic Course of the True Order of Studies Applied, Psychology, and Educational Philosophy, can graduate and receive the Degree of Bachelor of Scientific Didactics, (B. S. D.)

Students of any one of the courses of the College of Liberal Arts who will spend one year in the review of the studies of the Didactic Course, and pursue especially the Professional Studies, including those of the Fourth Year, can graduate and receive the Degree of Bachelor of Scientific Didactics (B S. D.)

Young men and women finishing the Post Graduate course, especially if they have talent and good health, will be sought for to accept Superintendencies, Principalships, and leading positions in our Academies and Collegiate Institutions.

CALENDAR FOR 1890–91.

The Fall Term will open Tuesday, September 9, 1890, and continne fiifteen weeks, ending Thursday, December 18, 1890.

The Teacher's Term will continue for ten weeks, ending November 14. This term is planned to accomonate students who desire to teach during the winter, giving them the advantage of a Review Term, and the privelege of quitting in time for the Winter Schools.

The Winter Term will open Tuesday, January 6, 1891, and continues eleven weeks, ending Thursday, March 19, 1891.

The Spring Term will open Tuesday, April 1, 1891, and continue twelve weeks, ending June 18, 1891.

EXPENSES.

Boarding. The University provides excellent boarding facilities at the lowest price consistent with a good table and comfortable accomodations.　Table board will cost $2.$$ per week.　Furnished rooms from 50 cents to $1.00 per week.

TUITION IN THE COLLEGE OF DIDACTICS.

Fall Term of fifteen weeks, - - $12.00.
Teacher's Term of ten weeks, 10.00.
Winter Term of eleven weeks, - 10.00.
Spring Term of twelve weeks, - - 10.00.

Let it be understood that there are no other charges than this tuition in this College, that is, there are no "Incidental Fee" or "Matriculation Fee" as some other schools require.　The payment of tuition is strictly in advance.　Students will not be received for less time than the full term, and no deduction of tuition will be made for absence either at the beginning or close of term, except in case of the prolonged sickness of the student or friends of the family.

GENERAL STATEMENTS.

1.　Who will be admitted?　Any of either sex, provided they are not too young or not too poor in scholarship to enter on our course of study.

2.　Students will be accepted for one term with welcome.　This term can be occupied in review of common branches.

3.　The student's individual preferences will be carefully considered and complied with as far as possible.

4.　Will a student be required to take an entrance examination? No.　Only a suitable matriculation paper will be made out.

5.　Will a student be permitted to choose his own studies?　Yes, within certain limits.　Each student, before determining his studies will confer with the dean, and when made aware of his own real wants and the class organization within the school, will then be permitted to decide for himself.

6.　Students arriving in the city should keep their checks for baggage, take the Electric cars on Fourth street, for the Union Stock Yards and then the Motor Line near the Stock Yards to the University at Morningside.　There they will be welcomed by the President or some other member of the faculty and given such information and counsel as may be needed.

7.　Students designing to board in the University Hall should write in advance to the University of the Northwest and secure rooms, then on their arrival they will be settled at once.　Students who have once engaged rooms and for some reason have given up coming; should kindly notify the secretary of the University of this change of intention.

HIGH SCHOOL GRADUATES.

High School graduates are invited to the College of Didactics with the privilege of choosing what subjects they may most need from the Didactic course. * They are requested to bring with them a record of their standing while at the school from which they came. This will be accepted, as the general rule. We do not flatter certain schools by publisning a list of acceptance. There are but few high schools in Iowa, whose graduates when coming here will not be heartily welcomed and accredited with the standing which they bring. This class of students need a thorough review of the early branches of their course, an. organization, as it were, of the elements of knowledge which they have previously acquired. There is no way so favorable to them as to enter the standard classes of the College. They will observe the mental conditions of their fellow students who have not had high school advantages, and if attentive in observation they will draw much information from their associates which could not be obtained if separated from the general body. Some high school students can take their degrees in one year; others may need to take two, and if they wish to enter upon the study of the languages, as German or Latin, or to become more thorough in some sciences, they may remain three.

Certainly these opportunities are equal to those offered by any other school, denominational or state. Be it remembered that all graduates of the College of Didactics go out under the same conditions, with the same degrees obtained by participation in the same course of study as are obtained at State Normal Schools.

For further information respecting the College of Didactics, address. J. C. GILCHRIST, Dean.

COLLEGE OF LAW.

FACULTY.

WILMOT WHITFILD, D. D., President.
    Lecturer on Medical Jurisprudence.

....Dean,

    Lecturer on ....
EDWIN J. STASON, L. L. B., Secretary,
      Professor of Contracts and Torts.
J. W. HALLAM, L. L. B., Professor of Real Property and Equity.

....

    Professor of Pleading, Practice and Evidence.

....

  Professor of Constitutional History, International and
      Constitutional Law and Political Science.

SPECIAL LECTURERS.

HON. GIFFORD S. ROBINSON, (Justice of the Supreme Court,)
      Lecturer on Constitutional Limitations.
HON. G. W. WAKEFIELD, (Judge of the District Court,)
      Lecturer on Conflict of Laws.
HON. C. H. LEWIS, (Judge of the District Court),
     Lecturer on Preparation and Trial of Causes.
HON. E. H. HUBBARD, Lecturer on Extraordinary Legal Remedies.

....

  Lecturer on Conveyancing and Examining of Titles.
C. L. WRIGHT,   Lecturer on Corporations.
W. E. GANTT,   Lecturer on Federal Jurisprudence.

....

      Lecturer on Criminal Law.
A. L. HUDSON, L, L. B.,   Lecturer on Evidence.
A. S. WILSON,   Lecturer on Insurance Law.
A. F. CALL,   Lecturer on Legal Study and Ethics.

College of Law.

CALENDAR.

The course of instruction will extend through a period of two years of thirty-six weeks each. (Period of study required for admission to practice in the State of Iowa.)

1890—Fall Term begins, Monday, Sept. 13.

—Fall Term ends, Friday, Dec. 19.—14 weeks.

1891—Winter Term begins, Monday, Jan. 5.

—Winter Term ends, Friday, March 27.—12 weeks.

—Spring Term begins, Monday, April 6.

—Spring Term ends, Thursday, June 11.—10 weeks.

LOCATION.

It must be conceded that as a location for a Law School Sioux City has few superiors in the west. Two terms of the Federal Court and five terms of the District Court are held here during the year, enabling the student to attend their sessions for almost one half the time. The amount of legal business transacted in Sioux City has built up a local bar equal in number and ability to that of any city of equal size in the country. Students have therefore unusual advantages for observing actual practice in the courts. They have the advantage of becoming familiar with practice in Dakota and Nebraska as well as in Iowa in the offices of attorneys who transact business and conduct many important cases in those states by reason of the fact that Sioux City is located practically on their borders.

The day sessions of the Law School will be held at such times as will enable students to employ the greater part of their time in offices, if they should see fit to do so.

COURSE OF INSTRUCTION.

The following schedule presents the course substantially as it will be given during the coming year.

JUNIOR YEAR—FALL TERM.

FIRST SESSION.

Elementary Law—Recitations and Lectures.
Contracts: General Principles—Recitations and Lectures.
Contracts: ,Agency, Partnership and Civil Corporations—Recitations.

SECOND SESSION.

Legal Study and Ethics—Lectures.
Common Law—Lectures.
Use of Legal Decisions and Preparation of Legal Briefs—Lectures.
Domestic Relations—Recitations and Lectures.
Negotiable Instruments and Commercial Law—Recitations and Lectures.

WINTER TERM.

FIRST SESSION.

Contracts: Guaranty and Suretyship; Contracts for Service; Bailments; Patents and Copyrights; Trade-marks; Insurance; Construction and Interpretation; Law of Place; Defenses; Statute of Frauds; Statute of Limitations; Interest and Usury; Bankruptcy and Insolvency—Recitations.

SECOND SESSION.

Negotiable Instruments and Commercial Law—Recitations and Lectures.
Personal Property: Sales and Chattel Mortgages—Recitations and Lectures.
Probate Law and Practice—Lectures.

SPRING TERM.

FIRST SESSION.

Torts—Recitations.

SECOND SESSION.

Criminal Law—Recitations and Lectures.
Railways and Common Carriers—Recitations and Lectures.

SENIOR YEAR—FALL TERM.

FIRST SESSION.

Evidence—Recitations.
Real Property—Recitations.

SECOND SESSION.

Common Law Pleading—Recitations.
Code Pleading—Recitations.
Criminal Practice and Procedure—Lectures.

WINTER TERM.

FIRST SESSION.

Real Property—Recitations.
Conveyancing and Examining of Titles—Lectures.

SECOND SESSION.

Preparation and Trial of Causes—Lectures.
Extraordinary Legal Remedies, Judgments and Executions—
Lectures.
Damages—Recitations.
Municipal Corporations—Lectures.

SPRING TERM.

FIRST SESSION.

Equity Jurisprudence—Recitations.
Liens—Recitations and Lectures.
Specific Performance—Recitations.

SECOND SESSION.

Constitutional Limitations—Lectures.
Federal Jurisprudence—Lectures.
Conflict of Laws—Lectures.
Drafting Legal Instruments—Lectures.

The course of instruction set forth above will occupy the entire
time during two school years allowing for two sessions of each class
five days in a week. In addition to this, instruction will be given
during the junior year on Roman Law, Public International Law and
Medical Jurisprudence, and during the senior year, upon Constitutional
Law, Political and Social Science, and Mining Law. Attendance

upon the instruction in Constitutional Law is required.   The remaining subjects are optional.

TEXT BOOKS.

The following is a list of text books to be used during the course:

JUNIOR YEAR.	SENIOR YEAR.
Law Dictionary: Bouvier.	Evidence: Greenlief, Vol. I.
Elementary Law: Walker.	Common Law Pleading: Gould.
Contracts: Anson and Parsons.	Code Pleading: Bliss.
Torts: Cooley.	Real Property: Washburn.
Roman Law: Morey.	Equity: Bispham.
International Law: Woolsey.	Code of Iowa.
Criminal Law: Washburn.	Constitutional Law: Cooley.
Bills and Notes: Benjamin's Chalmer.	

Arrangements will be made to furnish law books to students at reduced prices.

MOOT COURTS.

Sessions of Moot Court will be held once a week commencing with the winter term of the junior year and continuing through to the end of the course.   A statement of facts will be prepared by the faculty upon which the students shall prepare pleadings to be filed and briefs to be submitted prior to argument.   After the Junior Class has had Evidence the students will be required to prove the facts assigned by competent witnesses, submit instruction and make their arguments to a jury.   The jury trials will be presided over by the Lecturer on the Preparation and Trial of Causes.   Practice in the Moot Court will be subject to rules provided by the Faculty.

ADMISSION.

Students will be admitted to the Law School at any time during the year.   Applicants will be expected to furnish satisfactory evidence of good moral character and of a good English education.   The diploma of any reputable college, academy or high school, will be received as evidence of the latter.   All applicants who are candidates for a degree, are requested to call at the office of the Secretary on the Saturday preceding the opening of school for the purpose of passing such examinations as may be required.

DEGREE.

All students who are over twenty-one years of age and who complete the course and pass a satisfactory examination, will be entitled to a diploma and the degree of Bachelor of Laws.

EXPENSES.

The tuition fee will be $50.00 per year or $20.00 per term, payable in advance. Graduation fee and diploma, $5.00. There will be no incidental charges.

Special students may attend the lectures and recitations on any one or more subjects upon the payment of such fees as may be determined by the Faculty.

If a sfficient number of students desire it, instruction will be given, for a reasonable charge, during evenings throughout the two years, covering the ground included in the regular course---such instruction will be open to the regular students of the Law School.

For further information concerning the Law School, address the Secretary, Edwin J. Stason, Room 15, Metropolitan Block, Sioux City, Iowa.

CONSERVATORY OF MUSIC.
FACULTY.

MRS. EMILIE MALLORY,

Pianist and Organist.

MISS CARRIE B: OSGOOD,

Vocalist.

MISS ALICE GUNN,

Assistant.

Conservatory of Music.

GENERAL STATEMENT.

The Conservatory of Music affords facilities for a thorough and systematical education in the theory and, practice of music Special opportunities will be afforded to those who desire to fit themselves for the profession, either as artists or teachers.

METHOD OF INSTRUCTION.

Instruction will be given in classes and individually. The classes formed in Piano, Organ and other instrumental music, and in vocal culture are limited to three pupils each.

COURSES OF STUDY.

1. The History and Theory of Music.
2. The Voice.
3. The Piano.
4. The Organ.
5. The Orchestra.
6. The Chorus.

The full course of study in each of these departments occupies four years, but a student may enter upon any part of the course, for the pursuit of which he is found, on examination to be qualified.

PIANO-FORTE.

No other instrument of music is so universally studied as the Piano Forte, and yet we find comparatively few good performers.

This is due in part to carelessness and in part to lack of thorough and complete instruction and training. To remedy this, individual instruction will be given to each pupil by Mrs. Mallory, and beginners will be carefully assisted by Miss Gunn so as to avoid falling into bad or careless habits.

1.   Notation: including all peculiarities in writing, pharsing, fingering, abbreviations, etc., of ancient and modern works for the Piano.

2.   Time; including a systematic analysis of all Rhythmic forms.

3.   Technical Studies.

4.   Reading of Vocal Score.

5.   Reading at sight.

6.   Study of Tone.

7.   Accompaniment of Instrumental and Vocal Performers.

8.   Concerted Performers of Duetts, Trios, Quartets, etc.; for various instruments with Piano.

The æsthetic development will be made to keep pace with the above by the study of works of the best composers.

CULTIVATION OF THE VOICE.

In the department of Voice Culture instruction will be given in regard to the anatomy of the vocal organs and other parts brought into requisition in singing; in the use of the breath and the conditions of the parts necessary to produce good tone; in the fundamental principles of utterance as applied to singing or speaking; in reading music, intonation execution of trills, and running passages, and in musical expression.

⟋ Written as follows, viz: ˙

Vocal Physiology.

The Scales and Intervals.

Tune, Time and Tone Formation.

Studies of Vocalization.

Practical Metnods of Singing.

English Glees.

English, German and Italian Songs.

Church Music.

Church Singing.

ELEMENTARY INSTRUCTION, SINGING AT SIGHT, ORATARIO.

In order to encourage a taste for vocal culture, a class will be formed each term for elementary instruction which will be free to all students in the Collegiate and Preparatory Departments of the University. In this class will be thoroughly taught the elementary principles of Music and the art of Singing at Sight, after which the practice of Solfeggios and Chorus work will be taken up.

A class will also be formed for the rehearsal of choruses selected from the works of Handel, Haydn, Mozart, Mendelshon, and other great composers.

THE ORGAN.

COURSE OF STUDY.

School Organ.

Pedal Technics.

Pedal Studies.

Studies in Pedal Phrasing.

Fugues from well-tempered Clavier.

Sonatus—Mendelsohn.

The most careful attention will be given to the playing of church music and voluntaries; the proper use of the stops for Solo, Quartette and chorus singing; in fact everything necessary for a correct and refined rendering of this important part of the church service.

HARMONY AND COMPOSITION.

This department comprehends a perfect system of musical notation; the manner in which the major and minor tonalities are related to each other, and the relationships of the different keys or scales, also a thorough practical and theoretical knowledge of the intervals and the construction of chords, with the artistic laws which regulate melodic and harmonic progressions.

This course requires three years.

DIPLOMAS.

All pupils who successfully complete the prescribed course of study in any department of the Conservatory, will be awarded a Diploma.

CONCERTS AND REHEARSALS.

Among the very important advantages of the Conservatory are the Public Concerts and Rehearsals, which are frequently given at which pupils in the different departments, with the assistance of their teachers perform selections from the pieces learned at their lessons in the presence of their parents and friends, who have thus the best opportunity of judging of their progress; while the pupils are enabled to exercise their powers and above all to acquire the confidence which is so necessary to a creditable performance.

LECTURES.

Lectures are frequently given on Piano-forte Playing, Vocal Culture, and Musical History, with illustrations which interest and benefit.

EXPENSES.

Terms for Tuition for the Fall Term of twelve weeks, two lessons per week, payable in advance.

Piano-forte—First Grade (beginners) $12.00
All other grades .... $14.00 and 18.00
Organ... 14.00 and 18.00
Guitar .... 14.00 and 18.00
Cultivation of the Voice (singing) .... 12.00 and 15.00
Elocution...................................... 12.00 and 15.00
Private Lessons (one hour)..................... 24.00 and 30.00
Harmony and Composition...................... 6.00
German and French Languages, each............ 8.00 to 12.00

FREE LESSONS, ETC.

1. Class in Notation and Singing at Sight.
2. Normal Class designed for those preparing to teach.
3. Class in General Music Instruction.
4. Lectures on Classical Piano-forte Music, Vocal Culture, and Musical History.
5. The Conservatory Concerts, Reharsals, etc.

TERMS.

The Fall Term of the Consrvatory of Music will begin September 22d and continue twelve weeks.

COLLEGE OF MEDICINE.

FACULTY.

GEORGE W. BEGGS, A. M., M. D., Dean,   Sioux City.
Professor of Clinical Surgery.

E. HORNABROOKE, M. D.,   Cherokee, Iowa.
Professor of Theory and Practice of Medicine and Clinical Medicine.

JOHN P. SAVAGE, M. D.,   Sioux City.
Professor of Obstetrics, Gynecology and Surgical Diseases of Women.

J. A. SHERMAN, M. D.,   Cherokee, Iowa.
Professor of Theory and Practice of Surgery.

H. A. WHEELER, M. D.,   Onawa, Iowa.
Professor of Materia Medica and Therapuetics.

WILLIAM JEPSON, M. D.,   Sioux City.
Professor of Anatomy, Assistant to Professor of Clinical Surgery, and Secretary of Faculty.

J. H. TALBOY, M. D.,   Castana, Iowa.
Professor of Physiology and Histology.

GEORGE PARK, M. B., C. M.,   Sioux City.
Professor of Ophthalmology and Otology.

H. G. PITTENGER, A. M.,   Sioux City.
Professor of Chemistry and Toxicology.

M. W. WHITE, M. D.,   Sioux City.
Professor of Diseases of Children.

S. B. INGALLS, M. D.,   Meridan, Iowa.
Professor of Pathology and Bacteriology.

W. D. HASSON, M. D.,   Norfolk, Neb.
(Physician to the Nebraska Hospital for Insane), Lecturer of Insanity.

GEORGE JEPSON, LL. B.,   Sioux City.
Lecturer on Medical Jurisprudence.

W. S. THARP, M. D.,   Sioux City.
Lecturer on Genito-Urinary Diseases.

E. D. FREAR, M. D.,   Sloan, Iowa.
Lecturer on Dermatology.

S. C. HATCH, D. D. S.,   Sioux City.
Lecturer on Dental Science.

GUY C. RICH, M. D.,   Sioux City.
Demonstrator of Anatomy and Curator of the Medical Museum.

College of Medicine.

MEDICAL DEPARTMENT.

It has been the desire of the Board of Regents of the University of the Northwest, in creating the various departments of learning of the University to make them fulfil all the needs of a first-class institution of learning, and with this object continually in view, we have, in selecting our Medical Faculty, chosen such men as were specially fitted for the teaching of the various branches of the medical science. The majority of the faculty will spend the coming year in study abroad or in eastern institutions of learning, so as to specially be prepared to present their various subjects and to give the student the advantage of all modern views and advancement in the science of medicine.

The first annual course of lectures will begin in September, 1891 and continue for six months, ending in March, 1892.

In order that the graduates from this department may be well qualified and have a thorough medical training, attendance upon *three annual sessions* of *six months* each, will be required of all candidates for the degree of Doctor of Medicine.

OUTLINE OF THE PLAN OF INSTRUCTION.

Instruction is given by lectures, recitations, clinics, practical work in laboratories, dissections, and daily oral examinations.

The course will be divided into three years, Junior, Middle and Senior.

The lectures for the Junior Year will be on Anatomy, Physiology, Materia Medica, Chemistry, and Histology, with Microsocopica, work.

For the Middle Year, Anatomy, Physiology, Materia Medica, Chemistry, Surgery, Practice of Medicine and Obstetrics.

For the Senior Year, Surgery, Practice of Medicine, Obstetrics, Ophthalmology and Otology, Diseases of Children, Mental Diseases,

Medical Jurisprudence and Medical Diagnosis, Laryngology and Rhinology, Chemical Laboratory work in Toxicology.

Practical Anatomy in Junior and Middle Years.

Chemical Laboratory work in Junior Year.

Medical, Surgical, Eye and Ear and Gynecological Clinics, each week during the term—attendance required of all students.

TERMS OF ADMISSION.*

Students who begin their studies in the Medical Department of. the University of the Northwest are required to furnish as testimonials of sufficient preliminary education, a diploma from a literary or scientific college, academy, or high school, or a teacher's certificate of the first grade. Students who cannot furnish evidence of a sufficient preliminary education, are admitted on condition of passing an examination in writing in the branches of a good English education, including Mathematics, English Composition and Elementary Physics.

Candidates for advanced classes in the College must furnish satisfactory evidence of preliminary education and an amount of study and college attendance equivalent to that which has been required of the members of classes to which they seek admittance:

Graduates of Dental or Pharmaceutical schools of good standing will be admitted to the second year class upon passing the entrance examination only.

Lady students will be admitted upon same terms as gentlemen.

MEDICAL BUILDING AND HOSPITAL.

The Medical Building and Hospital will be combined under one roof the better to facilitate the Clinical and Dispensary instruction of the classes.

---

*NOTE—No student who desires to meet the requirements of the various State Boards, should hereafter enter upon the study of medicine, without an ample preliminary education, and the mental discipline its acquirement insures.

Such preliminary education should include the study of selected works on English Literature, Rhetoric, Logic, Mental Science, the fundamental principles of Algebra and Geometry, and the elements of Physics.

A knowledge of the rudiments of Latin is essential, since this in a measure removes the difficulty of acquiring the technical language of medical science.

IMPORTANT INFORMATION FOR PRECEPTORS AND STUDENTS.—After the year 1890-91 no graduate, unless he has studied medicine four years and taken three courses of lectures of at least six months each as required by the State laws of Iowa, can begin the practice of medicine in this State without passing a rigid examination before the State Board of Health. Every student who intends to begin the study of medicine, and wishes to comply with the laws of this State should enter his name as early as possible with a preceptor.

No graduate can hereafter enter upon the practice of medicine in Minnesota, Washington, Montana, North Dakota, Florida, or Alabama, unless he pass a rigid examination before the State Boards. And no graduate will even be admitted before these Boards for examination unless he has attended three courses of lectures of six months each. No one can begin the practice of medicine in Virginia or North Carolina without passing an examination before the State Board. Other States will soon enact similar laws.

The Building for this department will be completed in the summer of 1891, and will contain spacious lecture amphitheatres, chemical and pathological laboratories, and a large and well ventilated dissecting room.

CLINICAL INSTRUCTION.

The large amount of clinical material which will be offered by as large a city as Sioux City at the University Hospital and St. Joseph's Hospital will make the facilities for clinical instruction unsurpassed.

Further announcements of this department will be issued during the following year.

For further information concerning this department,

Address, DR. GEO. W. BEGGS, Dean of the Faculty,

or WILLIAM JEPSON, Sec'y, Sioux City, Iowa.

CALENDAR.

1890.

September 16, Tuesday—Entrance Examinations and Classification.

September 17, Wednesday—Fall Term Opens and Lessons are Assigned.

December 16, Tuesday—Term Concert.

December 17, Wednesday—Fall Term Closes.

VACATION OF THREE WEEKS.

1891.

January 6, Tuesday—Examinations and Classification.

January 7, Wednesday—Winter Term Opens.

January 29, Thursday—Day of Prayer for College.

March 30, Monday—Term Concert.

March 31, Tuesday—Winter Term Closes.

VACATION OF ONE WEEK.

April 7, Tuesday—Examinations and Classification.

April 8, Wednesday—Spring Term Opens.

June 19. Friday—Annual Examinations begin.

Jnne 21, Sunday—Baccalaureate Discourse.

June 22, Monday—Annual Concert.

June 23, Tuesday—Meeting of the Board of Managers at 9 A. M.

June 23, Tuesday—Meeting of the Board of Regents at 2 P. M.

June 23, Tuesday—Anniversary of Literary Societies.

Jnne 25, Thursday—Commencement.

J. M. POORBAUGH & CO.

PROPRIETORS OF THE

Red ⊙ and ⊙ Gray ⊙ Granite

Qnarries of Pipestone, Minn.

———AND———

The · Jasper · Quartsite · Granite

Of JASPER, MINN.

Their famous ledges of genuine Quartsite Granite are superior in quality and size and equal to the very best in the country.

The buildings of the University of the Northwest have been constructed of this rock by J. M. Poorbaugh & Co.

The Board of Managers take pleasure in commending the builder and his material. The course, dimension, range and rubble stone and work surpass any thing of the kind we have ever seen.

For Estimates and Prices, Address

J. M. POORBAUGH & CO.

PIPESTONE CITY, MINN., or SIOUX CITY, IA.

PHONOGRAPH
——AND——
PHONOGRAPH-GRAPHOPHONE MACHINES,

Controlled and handled in the State of Iowa by the Iowa Phonograph Company.
(INCORPORATED UNDER THE LAWS OF IOWA.)

Acting under Authority of the North American Phonograph Co. and Jesse Lippincott, Sole Licensee of the American Graphophone Co., with headquarters at Sioux City, Iowa.

PHONOGRAPH-GRAPHONHONE.
Operated by Hand, Treadle, Electric, or Water Power.

The utility of this invention at this early day can scarcely be estimated. The uses of this instrument with such manifold functions, would seem to be circumscribed only by the uses subserved by the property of sound itself.

As a stenographer it presents numerous superior features for that class of work, i. e.: absolute accuracy. It will prove to be the stenographer's and typewriter's greatest help as a time and labor saver.

As an educator it proves itself an important factor. Correct pronunciation in native or foreign languages. In elocution the modulation, tone, and other qualities are wonderfully and quickly perfected.

Authors, clergymen, lawyers and playwrights in using the Phonograph to prepare their manuscripts will readily be able to judge of the effect of their words upon their hearers. In these machines, professional men, especially clergymen and lawyers, will find a valuable assistant; they enable one to listen to his own rehearsals, to hear himself as others hear

MOTOR PHONOGRHAPH.

him. What the mirror is to gesture, the talking machine is to elocution; all tones of the voice, all its modulations, are reflected exactly so that every error may be discovered and elimintaed.

Either machine will be rented at $40.00 per year, semi-annual payments in advance. The machines have a speaking tube, hearing tube, oil can and brush, all other supplies are charged extra. Motor machines will be furnished with batteries, and the cost is about 4 cents per actual hour used.

The machines are packed and delivered at Sioux City, Iowa, F. O. B. All new improvements will be attached to the machines as fast as they come from the factories, without charge. No charge for supplies furnished to replace ordinary wear and tear, except the express or freight charges for moving the same.

Wonderland ———— ✳

Unsurpassed ✳ Summer ✳ Resorts

A Choice List of Summer Resorts.

In the lake regions of Wisconsin, Minnesota, Iowa and the two Dakotas, there are hundreds of charming localities pre-eminently fitted for summer homes. Among the following selected list are names familiar to many of our readers as the perfection of northern summer resorts. Nearly all of the Wisconsin points of interest are within a snort distance from Chicago or Milwaukee, and none of them ars so far away from the "busy marts of civilization" that they cannot be reached in a few hours of travel, by frequent trains over the finest road in the northwest—the Chicago, Milwaukee & St. Paul Railway.

IN WISCONSIN

OCONOMOWOC.	TOMAHAWK.
MINOCQUA.	KILBOURNE CITY.
WAUKESHA.	(DELLS OF THE WISCONSIN).
PALMYRA.	BEAVER DAM.
MADISON.	

CLEAR LAKE, IA.	FRONTENAC, MINN.
LAKE OKOBOJI, IA.	MINNETONKA, MINN.
SPIRIT LAKE, IA.	ORTONVILLE, MINN.
WHITE BEAR LAKE, MINN.	BIG STONE LAKE, DAK.

For detailed information apply to

ROSWELL MILLER, Pres., Chicago.

A. V. H. CARPENTER, Gen. P. & T. Agt., Chic.

E. W. JORDAN, Com. Agt., Sioux City.

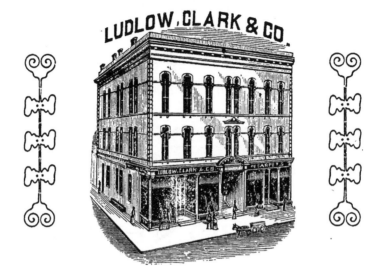

Dry Goods and Carpets

Fourth and Pearl Streets.

WHENEVER you are in need of reliable merchandise, at prices that are reasonable, visit our establishment, and we will show you one of the best selected stock of goods that has ever been exhibited in a western city.

We only buy goods that we know are manufactured in such a manner as a will give perfect satisfaction to the purchaser.

Each department is complete in every particular.

When you are in want of anything, if not convenient to visit our store in person, we would be pleased to send you samples, or goods on approval, to be returned at our expense if not satisfactory.

Our mail order department is in charge of competent peope, who will take the greatest of care that your orders are filled promptly and at the lowest possible prices.

Do not fail to visit our store, or correspond with us in regard to prices, styles and quality.

Yours truly,

LUDLOW, CLARK & CO.

CORN EXCHANGE NATIONAL BANK

SIOUX CITY, IOWA.

Capital, - - - $300.000.

JOHN C. FRENCH, President.
C. BEVAN OLDFIELD, Vice-President.
W. G. HARCOURT-VERNON, Cashier.

Transacts a General Banking Business.
Accounts of Banks and Bankers Received on most Favorble Terms.
Interest Paid on Time Deposits.

CORRESPONDENTS:

Seaboard National Bank, New York.   *National Bank of Illinois, Chicago.*
First National Bank, Omaha.   *Bank of Minnesota, St. Paul.*
British Linen Co. Bank, London, England.

DIRECTORS:

D. T. HEDGES.	JAS. F. PEAVEY.	T. P. GERE.
W. G. HARCOURT-VERNON.	JOSEPH SAMPSON.	F. W. LITTLE.
JOHN HORNICK.	C. BEVAN OLDFIELD.	JOHN C. FRENCH.
MARIS PEIRCE.	CRAIG L. WRIGHT.	

Collections a Specialty.   Correspondence Solicited.

'd.

7B/182/P